27.07

Winchester Public Library
Winchester, MA 01890
781-721-7171
www.winpublib.org

A Green Kid's Guide to
Gardening!

A Green Kid's Guide to
Composting

by Richard Lay
illustrated by Laura Zarrin

magic
wagon

visit us at
www.abdopublishing.com

Published by Magic Wagon, a division of the ABDO Publishing Group, PO Box 398166, Minneapolis, MN, 55439. Copyright © 2013 by Abdo Consulting Group, Inc. International copyrights reserved in all countries. All rights reserved. No part of this book may be reproduced in any form without written permission from the publisher.

Looking Glass Library™ is a trademark and logo of Magic Wagon.

Printed in the United States of America, North Mankato, MN.
102012
012013
♻ This book contains at least 10% recycled materials.

Text by Richard Lay
Illustrations by Laura Zarrin
Edited by Stephanie Hedlund and Rochelle Baltzer
Interior layout and design by Renée LaViolette
Cover design by Renée LaViolette

Library of Congress Cataloging-in-Publication Data
Lay, Richard.
  A green kid's guide to composting / by Richard Lay ; illustrated by Laura Zarrin.
      p. cm. -- (A green kid's guide to gardening!)
  Includes index.
  ISBN 978-1-61641-943-1
1. Compost--Juvenile literature. I. Zarrinnaal, Laura Nienhaus. II. Title. III. Series: Lay, Richard. Green kid's guide to gardening!
  S661.L39 2013
  631.8'75--dc23
                              2012023789

Table of Contents

Take Out the Trash!

Do you like taking out the trash? Nobody likes that chore! Trash is smelly and icky. But, there are many things in trash that a green gardener can use.

A gardener is a person who grows plants. A green gardener knows how to grow plants while protecting Earth. Recycling trash is one way a green gardener protects Earth. Recycled trash can be made into compost that plants need.

Not everything from your trash can be made into compost. Only things that were once alive can be used in a garden. If you make a pile of these things, insects, worms, bacteria, and fungi will come alive in your pile. They eat your organic trash and then poop, making compost!

Plants Love Worm Poop

Green gardeners do not need fertilizers made in factories to feed their plants. Green gardeners know that compost will do the job.

Compost is made up of decomposed plants. So it has the nutrients, or food, that growing plants need. Compost helps plants fight diseases. It also makes your soil come alive.

Compost has many creatures that can live, eat, and poop in your soil. These creatures make more places for air and water to get to the roots of your plants. And when they poop and die, they also add more food for your plants.

What You Can Recycle

You need many different kinds of food. But, there are some that are your favorites. Plants also need many different kinds of food. Their favorites are carbon and nitrogen.

A green gardener puts things that have carbon in his or her compost pile. You can throw in torn up newspapers, dead leaves, straw, hay, and vines. You can also throw in the bedding of pets like rabbits and hamsters. All of these are rich in carbon.

A green gardener will put lots of nitrogen in the compost pile, too. Nitrogen helps plants grow and make leaves. Nitrogen is in your leftovers from a meal, cut grass, and manure from pets like rabbits, hamsters, or guinea pigs. These pets eat only plants.

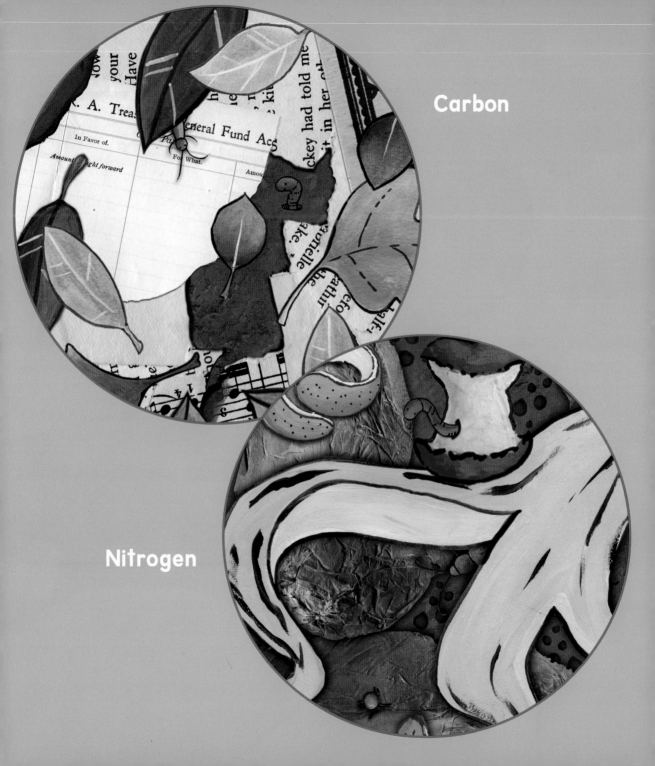

Carbon

Nitrogen

Never! Never! Never!

There are some things you should never put in a compost pile. Never put in a sick plant because it will spread disease. Never put in manure from a dog or cat. Their poop has bad bacteria. Finally, never put in meat, oil, or dairy products. That's because animals will get into your compost pile.

Getting Started

To start a compost pile, first pick your spot. You do not want your compost pile close to your house. Choose a place near your garden or even in your garden. It should be level. It should also be protected from your pets.

A compost pile can be on the ground or in a bin. Ask an adult to buy a compost bin or help you build one.

You will need other equipment to get started. A pitchfork or a manure fork is needed to turn the pile. You will need a water hose. You need a black plastic sheet to cover the pile. Finally, a bucket is good for collecting leftover food.

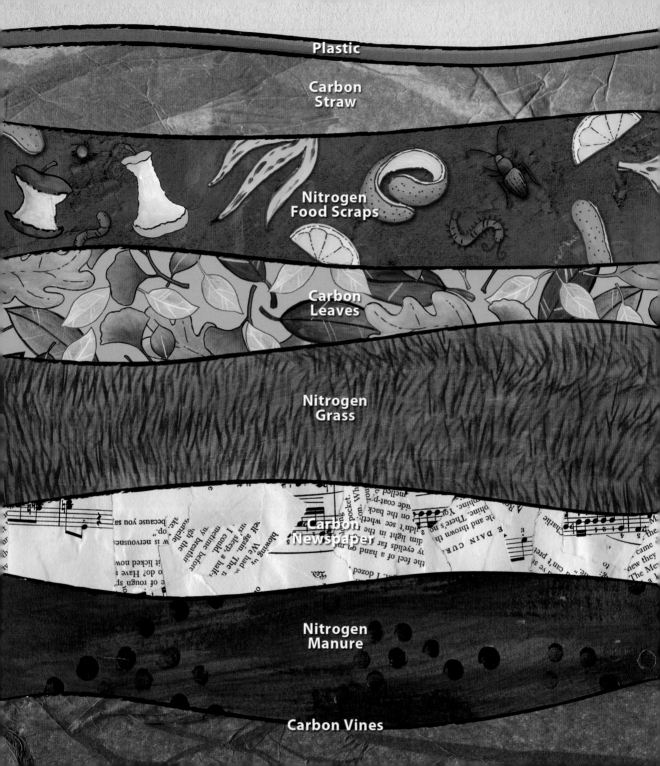

Building Your Pile

When you get your equipment, you are ready to begin building your compost pile. As a green gardener, you cannot just throw stuff into your pile. You must build it layer by layer.

Begin with a layer of carbon about three to four inches (8 to 10 cm) high. On top of the carbon put a six inch (15 cm) layer of nitrogen. Do not push these layers down. The creatures in your pile need air to live.

Next, add some soil or manure. These have the creatures you want in your compost pile. Then continue the same layer pattern.

When your pile is about four feet (1 m) high, stop. Cover it with a black plastic sheet. Now wait for the creatures to eat, poop, and change your pile into compost!

Keeping Your Pile Alive

Once you have made your pile, there are some things you must do to help keep your creatures alive. They need air. You can add air by turning the pile from time to time with a pitchfork or a manure fork. Or you can push a long stick into the pile in many places.

You need water to live, so do the creatures in your compost. From time to time, give it some water. Don't make it too wet or too dry. Both of these will kill your creatures inside.

There are three simple tests to show you have finished compost. First, when it doesn't look like the things you put in, it is almost done. Second, compost is done when it is dark and crumbly like soil. Finally, you know it is done when it smells like the earth.

Fertilizer Gold

A green gardener knows that compost is like gold. It is the best fertilizer you can use. If you live someplace cold, you only need to use about an inch (3 cm) on your garden. But, if you live someplace warm, you need more. The creatures inside the compost eat more in warm places.

You can also buy compost. Most garden or home improvement stores have organic compost. Do not buy compost from sewage plants. It is made from human waste and chemicals from factories. This will hurt both the plants and the people who eat the plants.

You're Ready!

You are ready to be a green gardener and make compost! A green gardener does not need fertilizer made from factories. He or she can take leftover food, newspaper, grass, and other plants to make compost.

A green gardener knows that compost is the best fertilizer to be used. Are you ready to compost?

Compost Research Projects

Group Project

You will need: Internet, 3x5 index cards, pencils

1. With a partner or in groups of three, make a list of 25 things that might be found in trash.
2. Using this book and the Internet, decide if each thing can be used in a compost pile.
3. On 3x5 index cards, write down each thing and whether or not it can be used in a compost pile.
4. Share with your class or with others.

Individual Project

You will need: compost, microscope, Internet, paper, pencils

1. View samples of compost under a microscope.
2. Record or draw pictures of any creatures you see.
3. Research each of the creatures you saw on the Internet and what they do in compost.
4. Create a foldable book of your findings: Creatures of Compost.

Glossary

bacteria: tiny, one-celled organisms that can only be seen through a microscope. Some are germs.

carbon: a mineral all living things are made of.

compost: decaying things that were once alive. It is used to make soil healthy.

decompose: to break down into simpler parts.

fertilizer: chemicals put into or on top of soil to make plants grow.

fungi: types of plants that lack green tissue, including molds, rusts, and mushrooms.

manure: the waste of animals or livestock that can be used to fertilize land.

nitrogen: an element found in the air and in the earth.

organic: of, using, or grown without chemical fertilizers or insecticides.

sewage plant: a factory that cleans the waste from humans.

Web Sites

To learn more about green gardening, visit ABDO Group online. Web sites about green gardening are featured on our Book Links page. These links are routinely monitored and updated to provide the most current information available.

Index